A Bite-Sized Brexit Book

I0463067

Farmageddon?

Brexit and British Agriculture

Edited by
Caroline Stocks and John Mair
Final Production
Neil Fowler

Published by Bite-Sized Books Ltd 2019

Bite-Sized Books Ltd Cleeve Croft, Cleeve Road, Goring RG8 9BJ UK
information@bite-sizedbooks.com
Registered in the UK. Company Registration No: 9395379

Bite-Sized Books Ltd Cleeve Croft, Cleeve Road, Goring RG8 9BJ UK
information@bite-sizedbooks.com
Registered in the UK. Company Registration No: 9395379
ISBN: 9781080479702

Acknowledgements

A chance conversation prompted the idea for this book, with Caroline Stocks lending her agricultural knowledge and time to the Bite-Sized Books Brexit team to see it brought into reality. John Mair provided welcome support as the book's co-editor, Neil Fowler helped with the subbing and it was published by Paul Davies.

Like the other books in the series, this volume would not have been possible without the help of our expert writers. As with the editors, they gave their help without payment and against very tight deadlines. We are very grateful for their contributions.

Caroline Stocks, Derby

John Mair, Oxford

The Editors

Caroline Stocks is an award-winning agricultural journalist with more than 15 years' experience writing about food, farming and the environment for national and international publications. Having graduated from the University of Sheffield with degrees in Journalism and Political Communication, she switched from writing about politics to farming after being asked to cover the development of a government food policy. After working for leading industry titles including *Farmers Weekly* and *Farmers Guardian*, Caroline was awarded a prestigious Nuffield Farming Scholarship in 2010, during which she travelled the world investigating developments in agricultural communications. She now works as a freelance reporter, has been a lecturer in political journalism at Derby University, and is a director of the British Guild of Agricultural Journalists.

John Mair has taught journalism at the Universities of Coventry, Kent, Northampton, Brunel, Edinburgh Napier, Guyana and the Communication University of China. He edited 26 'hackademic' volumes over the last eight years on subjects ranging from trust in television, the health of investigative journalism, reporting the 'Arab Spring', to three volumes on the Leveson Inquiry. John also created the Coventry Conversations, which attracted 350 media movers and shakers to Coventry University. Since then, he has launched the Northampton Chronicles, Media Mondays at Napier, and most recently the Harrow Conversations at Westminster University. In a previous life, he was an award-winning producer/director for the BBC, ITV and Channel 4, and a secondary school teacher.

Contents

Foreword

Farmageddon: Why Brexit could spell the end for so many UK farmers

Bio-Waste Spreader (Stephen Carr)

It is hard to imagine a farm policy more idiotic than the current Common Agricultural Policy (CAP). Since 2005, the EU has paid out €64bn a year of taxpayers' money to farmers for doing nothing more than occupy their land. To receive this money from the CAP's 'Basic Payment Scheme', farmland 'occupiers' have not been required to reduce greenhouse gas emissions or other forms of farm pollution, reverse the decline of flora and fauna on their land, or even produce food.

So why is there such intense anxiety in the UK, reflected in the apocalyptic title of this book, about what the repatriation of UK farm policy post-Brexit might lead to? Could a UK-devised policy possibly be any worse than the current CAP?

It is appropriate that the following pages give space to contributors from both Scotland and Wales. An important aspect of the difficulty of regaining responsibility for farm policy is that, for the first time, it will give the UK's devolved assemblies and national governments an opportunity to develop their own. Powers to develop separate policies were granted decades ago but have not been exercised to any important degree because the CAP (as its name suggests) has imposed a 'common' farm policy across the whole of the EU.

But with the CAP on the way out, the SNP government in Holyrood in particular has been toying with radical farm policy departures from those proposed by politicians in Westminster, including special assistance for new entrants and the introduction of livestock headage payments. The political relationship between the SNP government in Scotland and the Tory administration in Westminster has become increasingly toxic, as only Westminster politicians have been negotiating the UK's future trading relationship with the EU and other potential trading partners. Both the UK's national governments and regional assemblies are determined that Brexit should not result in a Westminster grab back of formerly devolved powers. Developing their own agricultural policies will be an important test of their ability to exercise hard-won political autonomy.

For UK farmers, the consequences of this political stand-off could result in farm policy anarchy. How, for instance, could English beef and sheep farmers compete with their Scottish counterparts if substantial livestock headage payments were introduced in Scotland but not in England?

Michael Gove, Secretary of State at the Department for the Environment and Rural Affairs (Defra), has finally conceded that he does not have the power to devise a UK-wide farm policy. Nonetheless he has advocated a 'Green Brexit' and drafted an Agricultural Bill for England that he hopes will set the tone and direction of policy for the whole of the UK.

Gove's bill talks of investment in R&D and making the UK a 'world leader' in food production standards. It proposes to fade out all EU subsidies and replace them with a vague policy that is centred around the principle of 'public money (subsidy) for public goods (environmental improvements)', and the nerdy concept of 'natural capital' that only Gove and his consultants understand.

On food security, the bill is deafeningly silent. A no-deal Brexit would present UK farmers with daunting tariffs on anything they currently send to the EU, although the damage would be limited because the quantities of food that the UK exports to the EU are very small. Apart from lamb and modest tonnages of malting barley (for brewing lager) the UK is a net importer of just about every other food commodity.

More damaging (although not to shoppers) would be the importation of cheap food as WTO trade rules replaced those of the EU. All sectors of UK agriculture would be sensitive to any cuts in import tariffs because hardly any UK farms are large enough, have a sufficiently ideal climate, low enough wages or weak enough currency to make them globally competitive. And even if UK politicians were minded to retain EU levels of tariffs to protect UK farmers from cheap food imports, it is doubtful whether they would be allowed to do so under WTO rules.

To take the beef sector as an example, the UK currently imports 40 per cent of the beef it consumes. Domestic production is mostly in the hands of small, inefficient producers who show heavy trading losses when unpaid family labour is attributed even a very modest wage. Other sectors like grain would fare little better. Even with EU grain tariffs in place, only a small proportion of UK cereal farmers (probably less than 10 per cent) make a profit from their production. Without protective tariffs the UK farmgate price of grain would drop by about one third (in the case of wheat from £150 down to £100 per tonne).

Even under the auspices of the CAP, UK food self-sufficiency has declined from 74 per cent to 60 per cent over the past 30 years, and what remains of UK production is alarmingly dependent on seasonal contract workers from EU countries. Food production involves dirty and often dangerous work. Long days and unsocial hours – particularly in the fruit, veg, and dairying sectors – compound the difficulty in finding employees. With voter concerns about immigration at the heart of the ongoing Brexit debate in the UK, the Home Office has proved depressingly reluctant to make any specific guarantees about how these sectors will source labour in the event of no deal.

Brexit – in enlightened hands – might have been an opportunity for Britain to shape its own coherent, interesting, dynamic food and farming policy; addressing issues like pollution from farming and improving farmland bio-diversity, promoting local food networks, even, say, reinstating Britain's regional farming heritage that has been so horribly distorted by the CAP. We might have kept current domestic food production intact by engaging in a sustained effort to protect the UK's domestic food market from ultra-low-cost food-exporting countries. The chances of this outcome look increasingly slim. It would need a determined effort by politicians ideologically committed to such a course and they are simply not in evidence.

As the next Brexit 'deadline' approaches, the Tory party is riven with political infighting over food trade policy like no time since Robert Peel's repeal of the Corn Laws in 1846. Such are the current divisions in Tory ranks over tariffs that Gove's tentative attempts to produce an Agriculture Bill have been kicked into the political long grass. Gove and the normally Europhile Chancellor Philip Hammond ended up 'spitting feathers' at each other when Gove suggested that many tariffs had to remain if UK farmers were to survive. With such deadlock in Cabinet on the Agriculture Bill, there are now justified fears that farming (which accounts for less than half of one per cent of UK economic activity) is simply being ignored as the UK desperately tries to secure bi-lateral trade deals in the latest run up to a potential hard Brexit.

Such anxieties are starting to affect individual farmers. The Royal Agricultural Benevolent Society says that even before subsidies and tariffs are cut, many farmers 'do not have enough money to put diesel in tractors or food on the table or pay bills'[1]. Adam Day, managing director of Penrith-based The Farmer Network, says Brexit has created an 'unprecedented ticking time bomb' and that 'the farming community is facing a perfect storm, and greater emotional support is going to be needed' (*ibid*).

However bad the CAP has been, it might soon look a lot better than the situation the UK now faces. There is a very real danger of potential farm policy anarchy, with UK food trade policy made up on the hoof or dictated by the WTO. Meanwhile, UK food production faces a collapse if farming finds itself starved of 80,000 migrant contract farm workers from EU countries. EU subsidies are also due to be removed. If 'green' payments to farmers are watered down or abandoned altogether, as is likely, as government concentrates limited financial resources on priorities like health and education during a predicted post-Brexit recession, then we will indeed be facing Farmageddon.

Notes

1. https://www.theguardian.com/environment/2019/mar/03/brexit-and-bad-weather-puts-uk-farmers-at-risk-of-suicide-say-charities

About the contributor

Stephen Carr has written for several publications over a 30-year career including, currently, *Farmers Weekly* and *South East Farmer*. Under the pseudonym of Bio-waste Spreader he has written the Agri Brigade column for *Private Eye* for the past 10 years.

Stephen also farms a mixed organic farm of sheep, cattle and some arable on the South Downs in East Sussex in partnership with his wife and four oldest daughters.

Introduction

Farmers were promised simplicity, but the reality of Brexit couldn't be further from that

Caroline Stocks

It's fair to say that UK farmers' relationship with the European Union is a complicated one.

With narrow margins in food production, many of the UK's 149,000[1] farm businesses rely on EU subsidies of £3bn a year[2] to keep their businesses afloat, while 500m consumers across the EU's 27 member states provide a ready-made market for the £22bn of food the UK exports annually[3].

What's more, thousands of migrant staff — largely from Eastern Europe[4] — keep farms running on a day-to-day basis.

To put any of these at risk would seem, as one contributor writes in this book, utter madness. And yet in 2016, that's exactly what UK farmers voted for.

Like the population in general, industry polls suggest the majority of farmers — albeit a slim one — wanted to leave the EU. And despite the more than three years of embittered debate which have followed since, similar polls suggest that feeling remains[5].

That might surprise those who know little about the farming sector. However, having been faced with increasing amounts of regulation — ranging from draconian pesticide rules to the downright ridiculous three crop rule, which aimed to limit mono-cropping in countries like Germany but had little valid application in the UK— farmers used their chance to say enough was enough.

In place of the CAP, they were promised a chance to tear up the rule book and replace it with a domestic policy which listen to their needs.

It would be supported by a healthy subsidy budget which matched the funding they currently receive — until 2021 at least — and most importantly it would give the UK the power to decide what was best for UK agriculture.

As this book explains, however, it appears these seemingly straightforward promises will prove difficult to deliver.

In his foreword *'Farmageddon: why Brexit could spell the end for so many UK farmers'*, written especially for this book, *Private Eye* columnist Bio-Waste Spreader sets out the challenges perfectly.

The existing CAP is by no means perfect, but creating a national policy — particularly in the midst of a political stand-off — will be neither simpler or necessarily better for UK farmers.

Trade tariffs, 'toxic' relations between the devolved nations, and a dogmatic focus on delivering a 'green Brexit' which favours the environment over producing food are doing little to instil confidence in the industry's heart. Meanwhile the threat to farm subsidies could be disastrous.

"However bad the CAP has been, it might soon look a lot better than the situation the UK now faces," he writes.

"If government concentrates limited financial resources on priorities like health and education during a predicted post-Brexit recession, then we will indeed be facing Farmageddon."

Having been at the heart of creating the domestic farm policy which may eventually replace the CAP, former farm minister Conservative MP George Eustice does not share this gloomy prediction.

Free from the clutches of the EU, he says the UK can reform agriculture in a way which encourages innovation, attracts new entrants and improves the environment, all while providing public goods such as improved soils and water quality.

A key caveat for success has to be around delivering Brexit simply he adds, which may mean the UK will have to align itself with the EU on policies such as pesticide use, but overall "UK farmers should be looking ahead with confidence".

In their chapter, *'The end of agriculture as we know it'*, Alex De Ruyter and David Hearne of the Centre for Brexit Studies express little of the confidence Mr Eustice has in the UK being able to extricate itself from the EU and the CAP in a simple, pain-free way.

Shared markets and standards of production have kept farmers across Europe on a level playing field whilst protecting them from global competition. But walking away from the EU Customs Union will leave UK farmers facing export tariffs, threats of border delays and weakening of standards, and potentially being undercut on a global market.

If the UK does maintain its trading ties with the EU, then producers will still have to adhere to the bloc's strict food standards and regulations; only they won't have any influence on those rules. It's an outcome that could change the very structure and operation of the country's agricultural industry, they argue, and not for the better.

Scotland's rural economy secretary and SNP MP Fergus Ewing is more damning in his assessment of what Brexit could mean for Scottish agriculture.

In his chapter, *'The search for stability and simplicity'*, he says Westminster has largely ignored the views of Scottish government and voters, leaving rural communities — many who depend on EU funding to survive — in limbo.

With the views of Scotland and the rest of the UK seemingly at odds, he suggests the only answer is for the two countries to 'choose separate futures'.

"I believe passionately that Scotland's future likes as part of the family of nations," he says. "[That means] our own seat at the EU's table, helping make decisions which benefit our people."

Guy Smith, deputy president of the National Farmers Union, uses his chapter to look at how trade shaped the farming industry we have today, and where policy needs to move next.

EU regulations ensure UK food is produced to incredibly high levels of quality and safety, but meeting those standards comes at a cost, he writes in *'Who pays the price for the food we eat?'*. Outside the protection of the EU, will UK farmers be able to afford to meet those standards, or should we look to produce less and import more?

As a country which is so heavily built on exports, it's a question Sir Peter Kendall, chairman of industry levy body the Agricultural and Horticultural Development Board, is quick to answer.

In *'Free trade and tariffs: An agricultural catastrophe waiting to happen?'*, he warns of the 'madness' of failing to secure a trade deal with the EU, and the 'catastrophic' risk of the UK becoming a dumping ground for low-quality food that UK producers can't compete with on price.

He does sign off with some positivity, however: "Land will always create opportunities for farmers," he says. "UK farmers are resourceful and prepared to adapt, so [no matter how the sector eventually looks] I remain optimistic for the industry in general."

In his chapter, *'Once a European farmer, but no longer'*, Yorkshire farmer Paul Temple picks up on this inherent entrepreneurialism of UK farmers to express his optimism for the future.

While he voted to remain, he describes how his experiences working with EU farm lobbying group COPA-COGECA revealed the true bureaucracy of EU membership, and why he now believes UK farmers will be better off outside the bloc.

"It will need more teamwork, cooperation and willingness to embrace change," he says. "In my book, that makes it probably the most exciting challenge I've ever faced."

Over in Ireland, dairy farmer Mat O'Keefe is far less confident about Irish agriculture's ability to embrace the changes caused by Brexit.

Ireland might be home to highly-productive, efficient farms, but the Irish border issue could bring farmers to their knees, he writes in *'A sector on a knife-edge: How a poor deal could leave Ireland's farmers as Brexit's biggest losers'*.

Huw Thomas, NFU Cymru's political advisor, paints an equally bleak picture for Wales' export-dependent beef and sheep farmers, who would feel the full brunt of EU import tariffs in the face of a no-deal Brexit.

In *'Silence of the lambs: How trade deals and tariffs could force Wales' sheep farmers to sell their flocks'*, he writes that the threats of Brexit far outweigh any of the benefits, such as streamlining policies, farmers were promised ahead of the referendum.

"With threats to market access and direct support, it's no exaggeration to say we could see some farmers decide to leave the industry in the coming years," he says.

After so many seemingly bleak predictions, we give the final word to Dr Viviane Garvey, an expert in European and environmental politics from Queen's University Belfast.

In her chapter, *'After Brexit - time for environmentally friendly policies'*, she discusses the potential for the new domestic farm policy to really deliver on the government's 'green Brexit' goals.

UK agricultural policy is at a crossroads, she writes, and the political rhetoric around encouraging environmentally-friendly farming practices could be a great opportunity.

For the industry to become more sustainable there needs to be a careful balance between the country's different farming landscapes, ecosystems and political priorities. Without it, Brexit risks being far more than a missed opportunity for all involved.

Notes

1. https://www.countrysideonline.co.uk/food-and-farming/contributing-to-the-economy/   ii.https://www.ft.com/content/0ee3cfbe-b5e4-11e8-bbc3-ccd7de085ffe
2. https://www.gov.uk/government/news/food-and-drink-export-sales-soar-in-brexit-boost
3. researchbriefings.files.parliament.uk/documents/CBP-7987/CBP-7987.pdf
4. https://www.fwi.co.uk/news/farmer-support-brexit-strong-ever-fw-poll-reveals
5. https://www.fwi.co.uk/news/farmer-support-brexit-strong-ever-fw-poll-reveals

Chapter 1

A chance to take back control of British agriculture

Leaving the draconian clutches of the European Union will give the UK the control it needs to create forward-looking agricultural policies which help farmers and the environment, says former Conservative Farm Minister George Eustice. He explains why the country has so much to gain outside the EU

I first stood as a parliamentary candidate for UKIP in 1999. My family runs a fruit farm in Cornwall, and having borrowed money to make significant investments in the business, we were badly affected by the high interest rates around the ERM crisis.

It was an example in what goes wrong if you give up control of your monetary policy, and it made me feel that if it was wrong to give up control of that, where else might it be more sensible to take back control of our policies and laws?

I left UKIP to join the Conservative party, and for the next 20 years was a committed to the argument of renegotiation — that we should stay in the EU but renegotiate the terms.

Prime Minister David Cameron's attempt to do that was a failure, so at that point leaving was the only option that made sense.

My view was hardened by being farming minister for over five years, and seeing up-close how EU regulation works and how it stops us from doing what we would choose to do as a country.

Farewell to red tape, rules, and risk of fines

One of the biggest frustrations of EU membership has always been the level of bureaucracy associated with it — particularly in agriculture — and that's something Brexit will radically overhaul.

Working in a department like Defra, I quickly discovered that any time you seek to change a policy lawyers will visit you almost immediately to talk about the 'disallowance risk'.

Disallowance is effectively the EU auditors' financial penalty regime, and the UK government is typically fined about £100m a year for what are basically trivial administrative problems.

Because there is this perpetual legal jeopardy hanging over Defra like a sword of Damocles, people become too scared to do anything at all. Perhaps even worse, that constant fear means that on a domestic level, any European regulations are enforced in a very draconian way.

Being free from that risk of disallowance means we can adopt a more common sense approach to implementing and enforcing regulation.

Generally speaking, the replacement for the Common Agricultural Policy (CAP) and the financial support mechanism we put in place will be entirely separate from the EU, so there won't be any EU audits.

The issue we will face is on things such as food standards, labelling and maximum residue limits on pesticides. If producers want to supply the European market then, of course, there would be a requirement to meet those standards.

It is possible that, as part of any free trade agreement we put in place, we will need to agree to certain regulatory alignment on things such as maximum residues.

But I don't think that takes away from the fact there would still be huge scope to see a different way of working with and rewarding farmers through the replacement of the CAP.

Creating a policy that works for British agriculture

Preparing to leave the EU has given us a once-in-a-generation opportunity to create a domestic agricultural policy which suits the UK, and it's been refreshing to be able to draft an agriculture bill that charts a course for decades of reform for the sector.

By moving away from an arbitrary, area-based system, we will have one which pays farmers based on what they deliver for public goods — things like the environment, habitat, soil health, water quality and animal welfare.

It means we can actually target policy and financial support to deliver on clear objectives, rather than just dole out subsidies based on how much land someone owns.

Alongside the change in the way we will financially support farmers, there are provisions to encourage the industry to thrive and grow.

There's a proposed grant to help farms invest, plans for farm tenancy reform, and a proposal to support farmers who want to retire while creating opportunities for new entrants.

Over the next ten years, I think we'll see opportunities for a new generation of farmers to come in, which will bring down the average age of farmers and potentially lead to improved productivity in areas where we've lagged behind our international competitors.

Managing the market shift

There has been much written about potential lost opportunities to trade with the EU, but I genuinely don't believe UK farmers should be worried.

It's most likely that we will end up with a divorce agreement which includes a comprehensive free trade agreement with the EU, so there would still be market access for our producers.

But even in the face of a no deal it would mean little change for most sectors, because we would have less import competition and producers would benefit from import substitution.

The sector which is most vulnerable is the sheep sector, because it currently exports so much to Europe. Having been closely involved in all of Defra's planning for a no deal, the modelling suggests Brexit would cost the UK sheep industry about £100m. However, the modelling also suggests that any tariff placed on UK sheep exports would cause lamb prices in Europe to go up by 20 per cent because we are the largest producer and import options are limited.

What's more, Defra has already developed a slaughterhouse headage premium which, in a no-deal scenario, would effectively compensate farmers for any loss of income on lambs they send to slaughter.

There are also other provisions in place to deal with the impact of a no-deal. The government would put tariffs on Irish beef, Danish dairy products and pork, as well as poultry from the Netherlands, so there would be tariff protection for British agriculture in a way it doesn't enjoy at the moment.

In terms of trade deals, the big opportunity for British agriculture is to have a better, more coherent domestic support policy. I don't subscribe to the idea that there are huge opportunities in international trade; by and large, free trade is a threat to agriculture's commercial interests.

For a country like ours, as the third-largest import market in the world, our opportunities are on our doorstep, and I think the real opportunity is through import substitution.

Obviously, it is important to have an export market for some products — particularly the fifth quarter, which is parts of a carcass not used in meat production — but generally speaking, the opportunities from free trade are far more modest than some would say, and the threat from other countries can also be exaggerated.

A model for modern global agriculture

An important role British farmers play is in their stewardship of the countryside, and I think leaving the confines of the CAP will allow us to do more for our environment.

My hope is over the next decade we can try to dovetail what I call the 'traditional' elements of farm husbandry — what my grandfather and great-grandfather might have done — with some of the best modern technology and genetics we have today.

For me, it's not about taking land out of production and farming the environment rather than food. It's about farming in a more sustainable way, and that's a huge opportunity for us to show the rest of the world how modern agriculture should look.

All while I was in government, and ever since I've resigned, I have argued that the ideal future for British agriculture will be one where we can deliver Brexit simply.

To achieve that I think we should rejoin the European Free Trade Association and comply with existing rights and obligations under the European Economic Area.

It means we would have some regulatory alignment, but I'm content to live with that if it means a frictionless border between Ireland. Most importantly though, we have full control of our agricultural policy, and that's a future UK farmers should looking ahead to with confidence.

About the contributor

George Eustice grew up on a fruit farm in Cornwall, where his family still farms, and was a public relations executive before being elected in as a Conservative MP for Cambourne and Redruth in 2010.

After serving in the Environment, Food and Rural Affairs Select committee from 2010-2013, he became an advisor to then-Prime Minister David Cameron on energy and environment issues.

George was made Minister of State for Agriculture, Fisheries and Food in 2015, a position he resigned from in February 2019 in protest of Prime Minister Theresa May's promise to allow MPs a vote on delaying Brexit if her deal failed to get through.

Chapter 2

The end of agriculture as we know it?

Brexit has the potential to change the very fabric of UK agriculture – and not necessarily for the better. Professor Alex de Ruyter and David Hearne from the Centre for Brexit Studies' explain why tariffs, regulations and a new-look domestic farm policy could come at a cost for UK farmers

Brexit could pose an existential threat to British agriculture as we know it. To many, including within the sector, this will sound like hyperbole. However, the reality is that agriculture as we know it today is fundamentally a product of state intervention and this is true both in the UK and across the world.

Leaving the EU has the potential (and we stress the term) to fundamentally alter the state of play in which UK agriculture finds itself.

This, of course, does not mean that we will suddenly stop growing things or raising livestock. But it does mean that the way in which this is done, the structure of ownership, the mix of activities and, as a result, the countryside itself, is changed utterly.

The extent to which any of this happens will naturally depend on both the outcome of the Brexit process itself, and the future policy framework of the UK Government.

To this end, we briefly outline three key pillars of European agricultural policy and outline how they might change post-Brexit – namely the European Union Customs Union, harmonised sanitary and phyto-sanitary standards, and the Common Agricultural Policy.

The EU Customs Union

Most of the UK's food exports go to the EU – £10.8bn vs £4bn to the rest of the world[1]. A large part of the reason for this is obvious: the EU Customs Union.

Most countries are deeply protectionist when it comes to agriculture and the EU is no exception to this. Consider the tariffs on a leg of lamb[2] as an example - the EU applies a tariff of 12.8 per cent of value plus €222.7 per 100KG on lamb[3][a], which gives a formidable competitive advantage to a British farmer exporting to France over his or her counterpart from elsewhere. It's unsurprising that 95 per cent of British sheep meat exports go to the EU[3].

These tariffs also mean, naturally, that British farmers are protected in their home market. The UK's agricultural imports show a similar story, with only a minority coming from outside the EU (of which the only significant bit relates to fish from Norway and Iceland and fruits – many of which just can't be grown in the EU or are highly seasonal in Europe).

Their removal would benefit consumers by reducing food prices, and there would be substantial pressure on any government to facilitate this in the event of a hard Brexit.

So, the impact of leaving the Customs Union would depend crucially on what came next. All options on the table expose the agricultural sector to significant risks.

A comprehensive Free Trade Agreement with zero tariffs between the UK and EU27 is one possibility, although agricultural exporters would need to get used to the additional paperwork (and costs) associated with customs declarations. However, this would be within the EU's gift – the UK would have only modest leverage in such negotiations and it's likely that the EU would drive a hard bargain.

Moreover, although such a move would enable further FTAs with other partners (about which we have heard a great deal from figures such as Liam Fox), it is unclear whether they can provide much benefit to the agricultural sector.

Most countries are highly protective in this regard, with China imposing a 15 per cent tariff on a leg of lamb, for example. Even with a trade agreement, many of these tariffs are reduced rather than eliminated – Switzerland pays a tariff of 9 per cent on similar exports to China (ibid).

Still, it could be worse – at least agriculture is spared the issues of 'diagonal cumulation'[4] that would bedevil the automotive industry in such a scenario.

Any new comprehensive customs union with the EU would at least guarantee tariff-free access to that market and avoid customs paperwork.

However, unless the UK were granted a seat in the table (and it's not clear why the EU would do this for a non-member), it would run the risk of having to open its agricultural market to third parties without any say in the matter.

Indeed, as in the case of Turkey and Mexico (albeit not applicable to agriculture) it would not even be able to guarantee like for like.

What is certain, however, is that under a so-called 'no deal' scenario, duties will be payable on exports to the rest of the European Union, potentially decimating parts of the industry that are heavily reliant on this export market.

As many readers will already know, differences in customer tastes, processing capabilities and various other factors mean that the UK will often simultaneously import and export different parts of the same animal.

Beef is a classic example: whilst prime cuts from an animal might be sold domestically, carcases are typically exported to the EU. Even though prime cuts are of higher value, the extra gains from exporting carcases can make the difference between profit and loss.

Similarly, mince is particularly popular in the UK and so the UK imports a significant proportion of its total consumption of this product. Since the UK market is highly integrated with the rest of the EU, at present this process is largely seamless and aids productive efficiency (as well as minimising transport costs).

Sanitary and Phyto-Sanitary (SPS) Standards

Common SPS standards are one of the key elements that facilitate frictionless trade within the EU and European Economic Area (EEA) [5].

Indeed, about 80 per cent of the time spent checking UK imports from outside the EU can be attributed to SPS checks. Any delay due to these (particularly on the Dover-Calais crossing) could cause potentially long queues and thus enormous problems even for non-agricultural sectors who are reliant on 'just-in-time' deliveries.

As a result, future SPS standards are extremely sensitive on a number of levels, and there will thus be enormous pressure for the UK to mirror EU standards irrespective of the type of Brexit pursued.

That being said, SPS standards are certainly going to be a major sticking point in any trade deals that the UK seeks to strike. Relaxation of these standards is near the top of the list of US objectives in any future trade negotiations with the UK[b].

Whilst the subject of chlorinated chicken has received a great deal of – probably unjustified – media attention, a far greater issue is likely to be hormone-treated cattle.

Whilst currently a banned practice in the EU[c], hormone treatments are common in the US and opening the UK market to permit imports of these will almost certainly be a top objective of US trade negotiators.

It is possible that relaxation of these standards will also be an issue in any UK-Australia trade deal, although this is far from certain and their use is not as common-spread as in the US. The scientific evidence on hormone treatments in cattle remains mixed and, since the possibility of harmful effects cannot be ruled out, the EU's "precautionary principle" dictates that they are not permitted. The use of 17β-oestradiol is of particular concern[d].

EU regulations concerning the use of antibiotics are also currently being strengthened on public health grounds (micro bacterial resistance) and if the UK wishes to maintain frictionless trade then it will need to continue to strengthen its own regulatory standards in line with these.

If the UK wants to align its food standards with the US then it will need to accept significant hold-ups in trade with the EU as the price of this.

UK agriculture would face a potential real hurdle on three fronts. Firstly, it would face extremely strong competition from farmers in the US, Australia and elsewhere.

It would also need to deal with consumer confidence issues as concerns over the use of chemicals in foods (as well as genetic modifications) potentially become widespread. As witnessed over BSE, this can be damaging irrespective of the scientific evidence or provable risk.

Finally, it would also face restrictions on its ability to export into the rest of the EU market, where SPS standards would remain much tighter. Any exports would need to prove compliance with all EU regulations, which would entail additional inspections and might be costly. It is worth noting that animal welfare standards in the US and elsewhere are also different to the EU.

The Common Agricultural Policy

This is the most difficult area to speculate on, as the UK's choices will depend not just on the future relationship it wishes to negotiate with the EU, but also its domestic policy choices. These would be constrained by any future trade deals that the UK chooses to do (including with the EU).

The protocol on Northern Ireland in the Withdrawal Agreement negotiated between the UK and EU contained several stipulations limiting the level of support that could be given to British farmers[e].

Future policy is likely to want to diverge from the structure of the existing CAP, which, in spite of improvements in recent years, still leaves a great deal to be desired. In particular, it has the effect of benefitting large landowners just as economist David Ricardo would have predicted in the 1800s[f].

In the coming years, it is probable that the UK will want its agricultural policy to evolve in a manner that promotes sustainable stewardship of the natural environment. However, there is likely to be a trade-off between this, changing consumer tastes and the amount that is grown domestically.

Doing so at a time when the CAP itself is likely to change further in ways that the UK no longer has much influence over will be challenging, particularly if barriers to competition from outside Europe (where agricultural subsidies are also far from atypical) are lowered at the same time.

The upshot is that the UK is likely to find its room for manoeuvre constrained at a time when the agricultural community finds itself buffeted by a series of outside pressures and the UK government finds much of its efforts concentrated elsewhere.

In summary, we would argue that the benefits to the UK from leaving the EU, particularly with a hard Brexit are likely to be few, whilst the costs are likely to be significant.

Notes – Numbers

1. HS code 02042250
2. The situation is a little more complex than this in practice: many countries from outside the EU have a tariff-free quota (Australia's is 19,000 tonnes, for example). Once that quota is filled then any further exports to the EU must pay the duty specified.
3. Diagonal Cumulation relates to so-called Rules of Origin, which stipulate how much local content there must be in the production of any particular item; for example, parts and components in a car.
4. EEA members are largely bound by the same regulatory framework as EU members and they are effectively part of what is known in common parlance as the 'Single Market', although they are subject to customs checks. Unlike EU members, however, they do not have a vote or direct say in those rules. EEA members are not part of the CAP or Common Fisheries Policy.

Notes - Letters

a. Her Majesty's Revenue and Customs. (2017). Regional Trade Statistics[Data set]. Retrieved 1 July 2019, from https://www.uktradeinfo.com/Statistics/RTS/Pages/default.aspx
b. World Trade Organisation. (2017). Tariff Analysis Online. Retrieved 1 July 2019 from https://tao.wto.org/welcome.aspx?ReturnUrl= per cent2f per cent3fui per cent3d1&ui=1.
c. British Meat Processors Association. (2017). Imports and Exports: Sheepmeat. Retrieved 2 July 2019 from https://britishmeatindustry.org/industry/imports-exports/sheepmeat/.
d. United States Trade Representative. (2019). United States-United Kingdom Negotiations: Summary of Specific Negotiating Objectives. Washington D.C.: Executive Office of the President of the United States Retrieved from https://ustr.gov/sites/default/files/Summary_of_U.S.-UK_Negotiating_Objectives.pdf.
e. COUNCIL DIRECTIVE 96/22/EC: concerning the prohibition on the use in stockfarming of certain substances having a hormonal or thyrostatic action and of beta-agonists, and repealing Directives 81/602/EEC, 88/146/EEC and 88/299/EEC (1996).

f. Daxenberger, A., Ibarreta, D., & Meyer, H. H. D. (2001). Possible health impact of animal oestrogens in food. APMIS, 109(S103), pp. S386-S401. doi:10.1111/j.1600-0463.2001.tb05791.x Retrieved from https://onlinelibrary.wiley.com/doi/abs/10.1111/j.1600-0463.2001.tb05791.x

g. European Commission. (2018). Draft Agreement on the withdrawal of the United Kingdom of Great Britain and Northern Ireland from the European Union and the European Atomic Energy Community.

h.]Ricardo, D. (1821). The principles of political economy and taxation ([3rd ed.] ed.) London: Empiricus Books

About the contributors

Alex de Ruyter is a professor at Birmingham City University and serves as Director of its Centre for Brexit Studies. His research focus has been in the areas of globalisation, regional economic development, labour markets and social exclusion issues. He has published more than 60 academic outputs in leading national and international economic journals.

David Hearne joined the Centre for Brexit Studies in 2017 as a researcher, having previously worked as an economist in a regional think tank. His primary research interests lie in regional economics and the sectoral and regional impact of Brexit. Ongoing research includes measurement issues within the regional economy as well as the north-south divide in Britain's labour market

Chapter 3

The search for stability and simplicity

Scotland's rural communities and farm businesses are critically dependent on support from the European Union, so much so that the country would rather walk away from the United Kingdom than give up its EU membership. Scottish Rural Economy Secretary Fergus Ewing explains why Scottish agriculture isn't prepared to deal with the complications of Brexit

With a mother renowned across Europe as 'Madame Ecosse', it's no surprise that I developed an understanding and appreciation of what EU membership provides for Scotland – probably much more than is healthy for the average 20-something.

My mother, Winnie Ewing, was an MEP for the Highlands and Islands of Scotland for 20 years from 1979 to 1999. During that time, she forged a redoubtable reputation as a feisty advocate for those regions' — and also Scotland's — interests.

Just as she left her mark on Europe, so Europe has left its mark on many of Scotland's rural communities.

Everywhere you go in our rural areas, you can see the positive evidence of our membership: the farming sector supported by more than £300m annually, the fishing vessels and harbours, which benefit from more than £100m of investment, the trees being planted in our national forests to help mitigate climate change, the £20m being used to fund rural businesses and community facilities.

All over rural Scotland, there are bridges, roads, sports centres, swimming pools, museums, art galleries, theatres, colleges, factories and enterprise parks, which have been brought into existence with support through our EU membership.

As the Scottish Cabinet Secretary for the Rural Economy, I now find myself in the unenviable position of trying to prevent the dismantling of that legacy, and to defend and protect rural Scotland's interests from the worst that Brexit might result in. It is not proving easy.

Working to ensure EU membership remains a reality

There are clearly pockets of rural Scotland where the vote to leave the EU was higher than in Scotland as a whole, and we need to understand why that is and to try and change that. But on any measure, rural Scotland's interests are better served by remaining in the EU than leaving.

That reason, and the fact that Scotland voted to remain in the EU, is why the Scottish Government is working to try and make that a reality — for all of the UK.

We published not one, but two assessments of the Brexit options to help add our views and analysis to the UK Government's considerations of what sort of deal to negotiate with the EU to leave[3]. Both were ignored.

We have engaged at ministerial and official level since summer 2016 to explore key issues and try and achieve common ground.

Given the potential impact of Brexit on rural policy, practice, law, and funding, Scottish Government officials in key rural areas like farming, fishing, animal health and welfare, plant health and disease, and food and drink have spent very little time doing anything else.

The fact that we have still been able to keep delivering a domestic agenda in the last two years – the full devolution of forestry, establishing a South of Scotland enterprise agency, providing grants and land opportunities to nearly a thousand new and young entrants in farming, supporting our food and drink sector to record turnover levels in 2017 – is testament to the dedication, professionalism and expertise of civil servants in the Scottish Government and our agencies.

And while engagement with the UK Government, and especially with the other devolved administrations, has been respectful and courteous, it has not resulted in much.

Scotland: The UK's expendable bargaining chip

We have a raft of statutory instruments passed at Holyrood and Westminster to bring EU law into UK and Scottish law in the event of a no deal. Despite the resource that has gone into producing and passing these, we hope we won't need to use them.

There are two bills on agriculture and fishing in the UK Parliament[1] that were swiftly drafted and pushed through the early legislative processes with unseemly haste, but by spring 2019 had been parked indefinitely.

A withdrawal deal was negotiated which ignores Scotland's interests on key matters like trade and migration. In fact, on rural issues like fishing, it is clear that just as the UK Government did on the way in to the EU, it intends to use Scotland's fishing interests as expendable bargaining chips on the way out.

The extension period to October 31 feels increasingly like an impasse; a hiatus that seems set to result in the same ridiculous brinkmanship from the UK Government that will draw us ever closer to the cliff edge of a no-deal Brexit once again.

And while any form of Brexit will damage Scotland's rural economy, all research and analysis suggest that leaving the EU with no deal in place would be disastrous. In food and drink alone, the cost could be £2bn – a sizeable chunk of its near £15bn annual turnover.

That is without factoring in what this long period of uncertainty, of drift and delay is doing to the myriad micro-businesses, often run by families, which make up much of our rural economy. No one can make any decisions about anything because no one knows what or where our future will be.

Since the outcome of the EU referendum, I have been determined that we should get on with making our own future.

In the last three years, we have pulled forward farm payments by using national loan schemes, to give farmers and crofters as much financial certainty as we can, pumping more than £300m every autumn into the rural economy.

Yet we do not know what funding will be in place to replace all this after 2022.

I have published a plan for stability and simplicity[2] – the most detailed in the UK – making clear that even if Scotland has to leave the EU, we will stay with the Common Agricultural Policy as it is until 2021, then introduce some streamlining and piloting of new policy and funding approaches until 2024.

We have spent the spring of 2019 discussing with fishing businesses and coastal communities a new framework for fisheries management – many of the measures will be introduced whether we remain in the EU and the Common Fisheries Policy or leave.

And through a National Council of Rural Advisors, we have a blueprint for developing and growing the rural economy sustainably.

Choosing a separate future – outside the EU or the UK

At the same time, the Scottish Government has made clear that we must have the right to choose our own future. We stood on a platform in 2016 that said a second referendum on independence would be considered if there was a material change in our circumstances – such as being made to leave the EU.

In fact, given the potential damage that Brexit will do to Scotland's interests, we would be derelict in our duty to Scotland's people not to give them the opportunity to choose a different future.

That becomes more acute when you consider the impact of leaving the EU on our people. Scotland's rural economy and communities have welcomed tens of thousands of people from all over the EU. As a welcoming and open country benefiting from the freedom of movement provided by EU membership, Scotland's population has begun to grow again. That is good for us all.

Every year, thousands come for seasonal work, helping to plant and harvest fruit and vegetables, including Scottish raspberries and strawberries. And many others have chosen not just to come and work here, but to make their lives here. They don't just take up jobs in fish processing factories, salmon farms, food manufacturers, distilleries, abattoirs, research institutes, and in rural hotels, shops and restaurants; they choose to stay in Scotland.

They and their families also support the wellbeing of our rural communities, helping to keep petrol stations, post offices and schools open in small villages and towns. And we are clear they are not just welcome to come, to keep coming but to stay here.

This also points to a divergence in values between Scotland and the UK as a whole. One of the UK government's key objectives in its negotiations to leave the EU has been to stem immigration and migration. One of ours is to prevent that from happening — to keep Scotland open for business and to people from all over Europe and the world.

When there is such fundamental ideological difference between neighbouring countries on a core issue which speaks to the heart of the sort of nation each wants to be, then it suggests the time has come to choose separate futures.

I and my colleagues in the Scottish Government believe passionately that Scotland's future lies as part of the family of nations, with our own seat at the EU's table, helping to make decisions which benefit and not harm our people and society.

That was what drove my mother Winnie Ewing in her time as an MEP for Scotland. She might have been the first Madame Ecosse in Europe – I am determined that she will not be the last.

Notes

1. https://www.gov.scot/brexit/
2. https://services.parliament.uk/Bills/2017-19/agriculture.html
3. https://www.gov.scot/publications/stability-simplicity-proposals-rural-funding transition-period/

About the contributor

Fergus Ewing is SNP MSP for Inverness and Nairn, a seat he has held since 1999. During his time as an MSP he has sat on various committees, including finance and transport, and has acted as Minister for Community Safety and Minister for Energy, Enterprise and Tourism. In 2016 he was appointed as the Scottish Government's Cabinet Secretary for Rural Economy.

Chapter 4

Who pays the price for the food we eat?

European regulation ensures British farmers produce some of the highest quality food in the world, but complying with those rules is expensive, and EU subsidies currently help cover those costs. Leaving the EU might give the UK Government a change to reduce payments to farmers, but one way or another – whether to farm businesses or the quality of food we eat – it could come at a worrying cost. Guy Smith, Deputy President of the National Farmers Union, explains the dilemma over standards and subsidies

It is not difficult to understand why agriculture will potentially be the most impacted of industries if, when, or how the UK leaves the EU.

The Common Agricultural Policy (CAP) is by far the most developed and significant of all the EU's policies. With its pan-EU support, it takes precedence over domestic policies at the national level, while the CAP swallows up around half of the EU's total budget.

Agriculture tends to be the most hard-fought sector when it comes to EU trade deals with the rest of the world, while the industry is tightly government by European laws, which regulate on hundreds of areas from food safety to animal welfare, plant health and environmental protection.

It's worth remembering here that the EU is not alone in this approach. Beyond Europe's borders, most developed nations also have complex and well-funded agricultural policies; from the US with its multi-billion dollar farm programme, to the Asian nations where the state purchase of commodities artificially underpins market prices.

The reason for this interventionist approach is quite simple: food supplies are too strategically important to be left to the vicissitudes of the weather and the market. Having said that, the importance of the rural vote and the farm lobby should not be forgotten.

The EU's CAP is based around three pillars — support, tariffs and regulation[3]. Regulation ensures internationally high standards in European agriculture in terms of animal welfare, environmental protection and food safety.

By way of example, let's take a look at chicken meat production. In the EU, broiler house density regulations require less-crowded conditions to raise chickens than, say, poultry farms in the United States[4]. There are stringent environmental licences required for broiler houses and rinsing chicken meat in chlorine as it enters the food chain is forbidden. This pushes up the cost of broiler production in the EU compared to countries where similar policies don't exist.

To provide balance to these tougher, costlier rules, EU producers receive support, either through direct payments, or through structure funds which include an element of trade protection.

From where should Britain be fed?

Brexit offers the UK the opportunity to design and deliver its own policy for the first time in 45 years. The question is, how heavily will it reform the EU's regulations as they are repatriated from Brussels to London?

To consider that, it is worth looking back through history at the way the UK Government has approached a national agricultural policy in the past.

A good starting date is the Repeal of the Corn Laws in 1846. There are parallels between the debate around Brexit today and the debate that raged in the 1840s, as it was partly about Britain's place in a world that was rapidly globalising with Britain at its centre[5].

Improvements in shipping technology (namely a shift from sail to steam) and the establishment of an Empire in faraway lands meant the reach of the country's trade was ever-increasing. But the debate around the Corn Laws was also about from where Britain should be fed — from home or abroad.

Interestingly, it was a debate that fundamentally split the Conservative Party, keeping it out of power for a quarter of a century. The repeal ushered in an age where international trade increasingly provided Britain's food supplies, rather than its own farmers within its own shores.

It wasn't until the Second World War that this approach was significantly questioned. The Nazi U-boat blockade suddenly made home production of food a political necessity as defeat through starvation became as real as defeat through invasion.

This fundamental change in thinking with regard to food and farming policy survived the return to peacetime in 1945. The 1948 Agriculture Act[6] ushered in a long-term domestic policy based on price guarantees and grants for agricultural improvement. This lasted until the UK joined the EEC in the 1970s with the CAP as described above.

The fundamental question now is should Britain return to its old pre-war fixation with securing its food security through trade, or should it endeavour to secure a percentage of its food from its own resources?

Accepting international standards – whatever they may be

If British governments choose to reduce support and trade protection, while chasing not to reduce the high-cost regulatory regime, then simple economics suggest we will increasingly be fed from abroad — especially if the farming power houses of continental Europe and the Americas continue to have policies more protective and supportive of their farmers.

At the moment, given the distracting noise around Brexit, there is still a significant level of interest as to the future of agriculture in a post-Brexit world.

When the American ambassador Woody Johnson announced that in any future US-UK trade deal there would be an expectation that US food and farming standards would have to be accepted, it generated an immediate debate in the British media[1]. Farming on its own might not be a significant part of the UK economy, but food and the standards it is produced to are of national interest.

At the moment the NFU is doing its utmost to ensure the high standards British agriculture works to are respected in any future trade deal. Whether this ambition survives trade negotiations and the strictures of the WTO remains to be seen.

Public money for public goods – but what is a public good?

Meanwhile, in terms of the future shape of domestic policy the Conservative Government has expressed a will to remove the £3bn support UK agriculture currently receives from the public purse by 2028[2]. Instead it will replace direct support with a series of environmental payments based on the concept of public goods for public money.

To the dismay of the UK farm lobby, a secure supply of high-quality, high standard food is not seen as a public good, but rather a market good. The bitter irony here is that while support may be downsized, and while trade deals may place UK farmers in a hostile global environment, there is an expressed determination from politicians that regulation inherited from the EU will not be relaxed, and that the resulting costs on agriculture will remain.

British farmers are proud of their high standards and do not want them watered down, but the prospect of freer trade with producers who comply with lower standards and enjoy lower costs is not an encouraging one.

Most British farmers would welcome a world where they compete with farmers abroad on a level playing field — one where all farmers get the same regulation and the same level of support.

However, they rightly fear the prospect of competing with farmers with lower costs of production, or those that enjoy a greater degree of financial support.

So, as I write, there is much for UK farmers to think about. Over the next 12 months decisions about standards, trade, support and regulation will be taken that could colour the fortunes of UK agriculture for a generation.

Back on the farm, most farmers would rather shut the farm gate on the games and intrigues of the political classes and get on with growing crops and raising livestock. Whether the future policy framework will allow them a fair chance to have that opportunity remains to be seen.

Notes

1. https://www.instituteforgovernment.org.uk/explainers/common-agricultural-policy
2. https://ec.europa.eu/food/animals/welfare/practice/farm/broilers_en
3. https://www.weforum.org/agenda/2019/04/when-history-rhymes-brexit-theresa-may-and-the-19th-century-corn-law-fiasco/
4. https://api.parliament.uk/historic-hansard/lords/1947/jul/31/agriculture-bill#s5lv0151p0_19470731_hol_211

5. https://www.theguardian.com/politics/2019/mar/02/us-ambassador-to-uk-woody-johnson-undefire-over-defence-of-chlorinated-chicken-post-brexit-jay-rayner
6. https://www.ft.com/content/db2a28e2-c175-11e8-95b1-d36dfef1b89a

About the contributor

Essex farmer Guy Smith is Deputy President of the National Farmers Union, a membership organisation that represents more than 55,000 farmers and growers across England and Wales.

As well as being a founder of the Essex Schools Food and Farming Day, he a past chairman of the Landskills New Entrants Committee, and a Fellow of the Royal Agricultural Society. He has also received an Honorary Doctorate for services to Agriculture from Essex University.

Guy is a columnist for leading industry titles including *Farmers Weekly* and *Farmers Guardian* and regularly appears on national media discussing farming issues.

Chapter 5

Free trade and tariffs: An agricultural catastrophe waiting to happen?

Promises of free trade and cheaper food post-Brexit may be helping politicians gain public support, but it risks destroying the basis of British agriculture if it allows the UK to become a dumping ground for low-cost, low-standard food. Sir Peter Kendall, chairman of the Agriculture and Horticultural Development Board, explains why leaving the single market would be catastrophic for the UK's farmers and food producers

About a week before the Brexit referendum in 2016 I sent emails to the organisers of the Remain campaign. I was worried that the Government hadn't been clear on the key issues affecting not just agriculture but the whole country, and — as a Remain campaigner — I was concerned we would lose.

Having spoken to countless farmers, many who actually voted to leave, I wasn't entirely surprised of the outcome of the vote the following week. But three years later I remain hugely worried by the prospect of what that decision could mean for British agriculture.

The British food and farming sectors have long relied on the EU. Aside from the support farmers receive in the shape of subsidies, nearly two-thirds of the food we produce is exported to EU countries. Meanwhile 70 per cent of our food imports come from the EU.

To put either of those things at risk by talking about leaving the single market is, to me, utter madness.

The European single market offers protection and support to farmers from unfair competition from overseas by placing tariffs on food produced outside the EU. Faced with a no-deal Brexit or similarly, if a poor deal is agreed, UK farmers could see those tariffs put onto their produce, putting them at significant disadvantage.

It's a situation which opens the UK to becoming a dumping ground of agricultural produce from around the world; food that is unlikely to have been produced to the same standards or with the same traceability we benefit from in the UK.

What's more, moving to cheaper food — something the likes and Nigel Farage and Jacob Rees-Mogg have repeatedly claimed will be a major benefit of free trade — will make a hard border in Northern Ireland almost inevitable. That's a constitutional crisis in itself, and it makes everything outlined in the Brexit deal so far undeliverable.

Destroying the base of British agriculture

Exposing British agriculture to unfettered imports will do what has happened only two or three times in the last 200 years: it will destroy the base of British agriculture.

Defra minister Michael Gove has said he is determined that free trade agreements won't result in cheaper, poorer-quality food flooding our markets.

But without regulation around that — which looks unlikely as it doesn't happen in any other industry sector — there's a real unease amongst the food and farming sectors that we are moving towards becoming a cheap food dumping ground.

I can understand the economics of saying that the UK could become a fleet-of-foot Singapore or Northern European-style service-based economy, and that we wouldn't make or grow much ourselves. But I don't think that's a scenario the British public were told about or want for that matter, and it's a pretty terrible situation for agriculture.

The question has to be asked, do we really want to break out of the single market? And if we decide to opt for a customs union instead — which would be better for agriculture — then why are we even talking about Brexit in the first place?

Brand Britain

There's much being said about the opportunity for UK agriculture to look beyond the EU for new and lucrative trading partners, and of course there are opportunities to be had around the world.

But we need to be wary of assuming we'll be able to walk straight into those deals once we do leave.

For starters, there are countless legislative hurdles we will need to overcome. More than two decades after the BSE crisis, for example, UK farmers are still unable to export beef to the United States.

There's also the issue of regulatory standards. UK food is known to be some of the safest and highest quality in the world, while there are concerns over both the production standards and technologies used in non-EU countries.

Where the difficulty will lie for the UK, however, is having the power to stipulate compliance these standards in any trade deal. There's no avoiding the fact that there are three key trading blocks in the word today — China, America and the EU — and if you are not part of these then you're a rule take, and not a rule maker.

Challenging sectors

A no-deal Brexit would be immediately catastrophic for all sectors of British agriculture. But if we look past that and assume we will secure a longer-term trade deal then there are still several sectors which will be under threat.

Many of the UK's farmers are incredibly dependent on financial support from the Common Agricultural Policy in the form of the single farm payment. The red meat sector in particular would suffer from any changes to direct support given that their margins are so low that much of their profit relies on financial support.

But when you factor in that export tariffs could be an average 46 per cent on lamb and 65 per cent on beef[1], it puts beef and sheep farmers under massive pressure — particularly once the Government's promise to maintain current level of financial support comes to an end in 2022.

When that happens I've no doubt the Government will do its best to prevent a complete collapse by introducing measures to stabilise different sectors. But what I've picked up through discussions with Defra is that it sees the single-farm payment being phased out, and that a lot of tariff protection will be phased out over a similar period.

That means at the end of the transition period, we could well see ourselves with no area aid, no single-farm payment, and significantly less tariff protection. It's at that point that I think the industry becomes unbelievably vulnerable to the peaks and troughs of global supply and demand.

Losing confidence, investment and skills

UK farmers are resourceful and prepared to adapt, so I remain optimistic for the industry in general – though I think British agriculture could look very different.

Whether they decide to rent out barns, take on projects around renewable energy or work in tourist markets, land will always create opportunities for farmers — especially when you think about the major challenges of population growth, climate change and dietary changes.

What I worry about is that in-between all of this we will have a series of peaks and troughs which will knock the stuffing out of the sector in terms of investment, confidence, and attracting the best people to the work in farming.

If we lose this critical infrastructure and see land returned to the wild as farmers leave the sector, then I worry that we will lose the productive capacity we have worked so hard to achieve.

In the long term, getting Brexit wrong will do damage to our farms and countryside, which I don't believe the British public really wants to see. But while a customs union might be the best option, I'm not sure that's something that will be palatable to those who voted to leave back in 2016.

Notes

1. https://www.nfuonline.com/news/latest-news/a-no-deal-brexit-must-be-avoided-at-all-costs-uk-farming-roundtable-warns/

About the contributor

Sir Peter Kendall is a fifth-generation arable and poultry farmer from Bedfordshire. He studied Agricultural Economics at the University of Nottingham before returning to the family farm in 1984.

He was president of the National Farmers Union from 2006 to 2014, during which time he focused on changing the image of farming to show that it is innovative, exciting and central to solving the world's biggest problems.

He was appointed chairman of the AHDB in 2014 and was knighted for his services to agriculture in England and Wales in 2015

Chapter 6

Once a European farmer, but no longer

It may have helped to lift farm profits and productivity in its early days, but today's European Union is stifling innovation, ignoring science and putting the environment at risk, says East Yorkshire farmer Paul Temple. Once a staunch Remainer – and former chairman of a major EU farming group – he explains why campaigning to remain led him to believe UK agriculture will be better off outside the EU

Before examining the impact of Brexit on UK agriculture, it is worth taking a couple of steps back to look at the impact of joining the European Economic Community's (EEC) CAP (Common Agricultural Policy) and reflecting on my own experience of working in Brussels.

From joining and throughout the 1970s, the effect of market management and support in the form of subsidies usually unseen by farmers had a dramatic effect in changing the shape of UK agriculture.

Incomes rose dramatically, while grants resulted in infrastructure investment that helped drive a dramatic lift in productivity. Many traditional mixed farms found there was more — and easier — money to be made from switching to all-arable systems.

This rapid change was welcomed by a generation who had grown up with food shortages and rationing; it saw them being provided with affordable food which, for many, transformed their standard of living.

It also began the slow process of increasing the income of those who worked in agriculture. Retrospectively, that success was clouded by ever-increasing surpluses, with politics far too slow to react to the productivity that new genetics and crop inputs had unleashed.

My own understanding of EEC agriculture changed from the moment I first drove across France and opened my eyes to the incredible power of the country's agricultural industry.

As a farmer on the East Yorkshire Wolds, I could appreciate what agriculture was capable of: I could see the importance of farming from a European perspective, and I felt a passion for being seen as a European farmer.

Inevitably, politics tried to catch-up with the food surpluses and the expectations that had been created as the EEC took on new member states and changed to become the EU.

Over that time I farmed first-hand through two major European agriculture reforms — the MacSharry and the Fischler reforms — which should have left the farming industry working with the market place. With each reform, we dramatically changed the way we farmed, quickly learning to adapt to the new system.

Eroding the European farmer

For several years, I chaired the Cereals, Oilseeds and Protein group of Copa Cogeca, the EU's farming group, and working in Brussels gave me first-hand insight to the importance of European agriculture and working together.

For me, it was always about the ability to trade freely, work with the market place on a common regulatory framework, to respect the environment, and make best use of science.

I admired many of the hugely talented staff in the European Commission, and in the beginning of my time there things got done reasonably easily. The balance seemed right and I saw myself as essentially a European farmer.

Two things slowly changed my perspective. Firstly, politics — and particularly social politics — increasingly got in the way of good farming and science.

As a sceptic of genetic modification, 20 years ago I took part in GM crop trials. Seeing first-hand the benefits GM offered farming and the environment reinforced to me how important modern plant breeding techniques are.

The EU's overly-cautious approach towards GM, however, has denied that science to me and other farmers. The technology and research have been driven from Europe, and yet millions of tonnes of GM-derived product are imported into Europe each year.

Another example of the EU's questionable approach to agricultural science is around pesticide regulation: it is removing many pesticides from use, but imports from countries which still use those products continue to enter our shores.

This anti-science approach has chipped away at my belief in the EU, as nobody can be held accountable for the decisions being made.

Building complexity

The second element which changed my feelings towards the EU was the change that was brought about through the adoption of the Lisbon treaty.

Bringing in the European Parliament fundamentally slowed down decision making, tripling the time taken to pass legislation and causing ever bigger issues as it brought increasingly subjective views into farming.

The drive for a greater federal agenda was not something that ever made sense; across all of its member states, the EU was never going to remotely resemble either the federalism of the US or indeed Germany.

In addition, the reform brought through by then European Commissioner for Agriculture, Dacian Ciolos, undid all the good work of his predecessor, Mariann Fischer-Boel, shifting it to a hazy, complex social policy which paid lip service to the environment.

Rather than address the inherent structural problems they had in creating sustainable farming businesses, many member states decided that pumping money into regions to retain votes was the easy option.

This has simply lead to many regions winding down farming and neglecting the vital relationship it has with the environment. With no prospect of a sensible income from farming, many talented young people have left rural areas, leaving regions devoid of youth and the wider environment suffering.

Campaigning to remain

So when the referendum was announced, I wanted to sit back and consider both sides of the argument before deciding if I was going to vote to remain or leave. Instinctively I wanted to remain, but damage to science and the decision-making I was seeing at first-hand was difficult to ignore.

Eventually there were three things which led me to vote to remain, and to actively campaign to stay in the EU. Firstly, however frustrating it may be, I am a believer of working together to bring about change.

The UK has genuinely been a force for the good within the EU; we are different and we bring a different perspective to many issues with benefit. I appreciated quite quickly working in Brussels of the importance of working on an equal level with both big and small member states.

Secondly, from a global perspective I felt the UK needed to be part of a strong trading block, with one set of regulations and one set of powerful trade negotiators. There is literally no way the UK could have that same capacity as one country at the relatively low cost of membership.

Finally, and somewhat prophetically, I stood on the border in Ireland in January 2016 and fully realised that the complication behind this border was the biggest, single, and simplest reason for staying in, as the politics behind it was too complex.

As events turned, I was a Remainer that lost, and despite realising the scale of the task ahead — much of which I would reluctantly be involved with — I accepted the democratic result.

The Brexit readjustment

As the process of extracting ourselves from the EU began however, I began to see things differently, and I've switched to supporting the concept of properly leaving for a number of reasons.

Firstly, I've come to realise there should never have been any discussion about a hard border with Ireland, as it is both impractical and unnecessary.

In fact, it's a suggestion the UK never talked about — this was the EU's version of 'project fear'. What it really amounted to was a lack of trust the EU had in Ireland in future cross border trade and traceability.

Most importantly, however, I realised from the moment the vote was taken that the direction for the UK and its farming sector was obvious.

Markets would be more open to imports, exports would come at a varying degree of greater cost, and financial support would switch to the environment. All of this is not necessarily a bad thing but comes with a degree of difficulty and readjustment.

We are, however, net importers — we have first-class retailers and a world-class food manufacturing industry.

For these reasons I could sense real change on the horizon, and I took two major decisions quickly, on the basis of it being easier to make investments while receiving financial support through the CAP than waiting for it to end.

The future would be about productivity, I realised; it would be about servicing the supply chain against greater competition and rising to the environmental challenge.

From a practical perspective, this encouraged me into the Conservation Agriculture approach of no-till drilling.

The environmental benefits were obvious, while the prospect of much lower fuel and machinery costs was a massive incentive for a tenant farmer.

Embracing the Brexit change

Now three years in, I've made plenty of mistakes but I have no regrets; I've found a new inspiring reason to embrace the biology of soil I previously had little understanding for.

The second major decision surrounded our beef enterprise. Much of our beef operation is tied into many environmental grasses, all of which would continue to need managing with the suckler cows we have, but in all probability with a lower income from the market place. We had two options: either get out or become more productive. I decided to accept the latter.

So we have set a new target of numbers: 50 per cent more cows, but with the same labour. This will need better management and investment in handling and housing. The investment is being made, with the new stock bull shed being leading us to ask why we didn't do this before.

The world's food supply is finely-balanced for many reasons, and post-Brexit UK farm produce will remain in great demand — possibly even greater than now. I genuinely believe the change Brexit brings to UK agriculture will leave it in better commercial shape.

Finally, future farming will remain about people; from the quality of their technical skills and dedication to hard work in difficult weather, through to the quality of the management we apply.

It will need more teamwork, cooperation, and willingness to embrace change. In my book, that makes it probably the most exciting challenge I've ever faced. I'm not sure of success, but there is a sense of past generations telling me to get on with it.

About the contributor

Paul Temple farms 312 hectares in partnership on the East Yorkshire Wolds, producing cereals for seed, oilseed rape, vegetables and beef. The farm has taken part in the GM Field Scale Evaluation trials and is part of the highest tier of environmental stewardship schemes.

Paul is the past vice president of the National Farmers Union, former chairman of the Copa Cogeca Cereals, Oilseeds and Protein Group, and founder of the European Biotech Forum.

He previously sat on the National Non-Food Crops Board, and is currently the chairman of the AHDB's cereals and oilseeds sector, as well as chairman of the Voluntary Initiative — an industry-led programme which promotes responsible use of pesticides

A sector on a knife-edge: How a poor deal could leave Ireland's farmers as Brexit's biggest losers

As a sector so dependent on export trade, Ireland's agricultural industry — particularly the beef and dairy sectors — will be plunged into disaster if the UK fails to secure the right exit deal with the European Union. Matt O'Keefe, editor of *Irish Farmers Monthly* and a dairy farmer in Kilkenny, explains why farmers north and south of the border are watching with trepidation

While the exact terms of Britain's departure from the EU are still not certain, Brexit — in whatever form it takes — will cause serious disruption to trade between the UK and Ireland, especially for the Irish agri-food export sector.

Compared to other export industries in Ireland, the country's farming and food sector has a far higher dependence on the UK market, and is therefore the most exposed sector to any negative economic impact of the UK Brexit decision.

In 2017, the UK accounted for €5.2bn of Ireland's agri-related exports — almost 40 per cent of total exports by the sector[1]. The beef sector is particularly reliant on the UK, where it sends more than half of all exports, while the UK market is vital for dairy farmers, with 22 per cent of Ireland's dairy exports heading over the border (*ibid*).

There's no doubt that in the event of a no-deal, Irish food producers would face a range of immediate and serious challenges — many of which a large number of farmers would never recover from.

Borders and tariffs

Without doubt, one of the most significant issues in the Brexit debate is around the border between Ireland and the UK. A hard Brexit or no-Brexit scenario leaves Irish producers with the threat of tariffs being placed on their food if it is to be sent to the UK.

In addition, there would be serious delays and increased paperwork to be completed as new customs and regulatory arrangements would have to be introduced overnight.

In the event of a no-deal Brexit, the automatic fallback position would place trading arrangements between the EU and the UK under World Trade Organisation (WTO) rules. That means the imposition of tariffs and customs checks between Ireland and the UK would automatically apply.

In that situation, those most immediately affected would be fresh food exporters with just-in-time delivery schedules to major UK retailers. UK consumers would also suffer as the imposition of tariffs on food imports would result in higher food prices on supermarket shelves.

In the event that a withdrawal agreement is concluded between the EU and UK, it is still likely that tariffs on imports would be imposed, though over a longer timescale than would happen if no deal is agreed. That would depend on the terms of any trade deal negotiated between the UK and the EU over the coming years and the length of time required to conclude such a deal.

While the UK would hope that a trade deal could be concluded promptly, the considerable length of time it took for the EU to complete trade deals with the Mercosur South American trade bloc — some 22 years[2] — suggests a UK-EU trade deal could be several years away.

Dairy disruption

Irish dairy farmers have been in an expansionist mode since the abolition of EU restrictions on milk production four years ago. Milk output from Irish farms has increased by 50 per cent since then, with the potential to double production by 2022[3].

The challenge has been to find new customers for this dairy produce and Irish exporters have worked hard to develop new markets and expand existing ones across the globe, particularly in the US, Asia and MENA (Middle East/North Africa).

However, the UK is still a primary destination for Irish dairy: the country accounts for a fifth of Irish dairy exports[4], representing 41 per cent of total

Irish cheese exports, 26 per cent of butter manufacture and 12 per cent of SMP (skim milk powder) production[5].

Last year, Ireland exported more than 80,000 tonnes of cheddar cheese to the UK, representing more than 80 per cent of all cheddar imported by the UK[6].

Ireland is the only significant exporter of cheddar to the UK market, and the UK market is the only market of significance for Irish cheddar.

Any disruption or increased cost on those exports would have serious financial repercussions for Irish milk producers as well as processors and exporters.

Glanbia, the largest milk processor in Ireland, calculates that WTO-level tariffs on cheddar exports would cost its dairy farmers upwards of €0.03 per litre of milk produced.

Other Irish milk processors are even more exposed to — and reliant on — the UK cheddar cheese market, with significantly greater financial impact for their milk suppliers if tariffs are imposed on dairy imports from Ireland.

All-Ireland trade disruption

The logistical nightmare Brexit could cause by disrupting trade within the island of Ireland is a major issue for farmers and businesses on both sides of the border.

For instance, the Republic imports almost one billion litres of milk from Northern Ireland annually. Around three-quarters of that milk is processed in the Republic, mainly for re-export, with the remainder used in the fresh milk market for immediate consumption.

The amalgamation of Lakeland Dairies in the Republic with the cross-border entity Lacpatrick Dairies earlier in 2019[7] further highlights the potential for considerable disruption of a highly integrated milk processing industry in Ireland.

If the UK crashes out of Europe there will have to be immediate controls and checks put in place which will cause delays, while potential levies or tariffs on dairy movements will lead to potentially crippling increased costs.

Even more frustratingly, there is also a real risk that farmers who sell their milk to processors south of the border may find that they can no longer do so. This is because under its controls to protect single market products, the

EU won't allow creamery tanks which contain 'mixed' EU and third-country milk.

All of these issues combine to heap serious concern on the continuing viability of this cross-border trade. But the loss of — or diminished access to — the UK market would not just impact the viability of cross-border trade between Ireland and the Republic; it would also have a destabilising impact on the overall value of the Irish dairy sector.

Potential beef sector collapse

While the post-Brexit future for Ireland's dairy sector is concerning, it's no exaggeration to say Brexit's impact on the beef sector could be catastrophic.

Ireland's beef sector is built on exports, with 90 per cent of production leaving the country's shores. Over half of that amount goes to the UK[8].

Market proximity has always been a primary attraction for Irish beef processors selling onto the British market, allied to the fact that Britain is the best paying market for beef in Europe.

UK consumers have eaten Irish beef for generations and are loyal to the product, after English or Scotch beef. Most of the major British supermarkets stock Irish beef and many of them rely almost solely on beef supplied from Ireland.

Geographical proximity also means that much of the Irish beef exported to Britain is fresh product, which British consumers prefer over frozen beef. As with Irish dairy exports, transport, regulatory or customs delays would severely disrupt this fresh meat business, adding additional costs and time delays.

Estimates suggest that increased costs and tariffs could effectively price Irish beef out of the UK market, in the event of a hard or no-deal Brexit[9].

Since UK supermarkets would be unwilling to pass all of the extra costs on to their customers, the financial burden would ultimately fall on the primary producer, making an already marginal enterprise totally uneconomic.

If Irish beef is priced out of the UK market because of Brexit, there is the likelihood of massive product displacement and price cutting across the EU as Irish beef sellers would attempt to find other markets on continental Europe for their produce.

As a mature market, the capacity of the EU beef market to absorb increased imports is low. Irish beef exports to the UK represent almost 10 per cent of the intra-EU beef trade[10], hence the potential destabilising effect on beef markets across the EU.

A precarious sector reliant on subsidies

Recent income figures for Irish cattle farmers, compiled by IFAC (Irish Farm Accounts Cooperative), show that a majority of farmers already rely on EU payments for a large portion of their income[11]. To help pay their bills many have second jobs off the farm, or depend on others in the family to bring in extra money.

Some larger-scale producers are marginally profitable, but without EU subsidies over 60 per cent of cattle farmers failed to make a profit in 2018. The average beef farm lost €116 per hectare (ibid).

These figures show the precarious nature of beef farming in Ireland. Any further deterioration in beef prices would exacerbate an already poor income profile.

Teagasc, the Irish Extension and Advisory Service, estimates that the imposition of WTO tariffs on Irish beef exported to the UK would deliver a severe price shock, reducing Irish beef prices by upwards of 35 per cent[13].

While beef finishers would be in the front line for these price shocks, the effects would percolate right down the chain to the calf producer, affecting already tight or non-existent margins on thousands of suckler-cow farms as well as dairy farms supplying cull cows and surplus calves to the beef sector.

Without massive increases in EU subsidisation, a hard Brexit would drive an estimated 15,000 Irish cattle farmers out of the enterprise within three years.

Since Britain would no longer be a net contributor to the bloc, the availability of extra funds to prop up the Irish beef sector, or the political willingness to do so by the EU's main paymasters, must be in considerable doubt. In the wake of the Mercosur trade deal, the EU is already preparing to allow an extra 100,000 tonnes of South American beef onto the European market[14].

With Britain exiting the European Union the additional supply pressures from South America there could be quite catastrophic effects on farmgate cattle prices, not just in Ireland but right across the EU.

Notes

1. https://www.nfuonline.com/news/latest-news/a-no-deal-brexit-must-be-avoided-at-all-costs-uk-farming-roundtable-warns/
2. https://www.agriculture.gov.ie/brexit/tradeandstatistics/
3. https://www.euronews.com/2019/07/03/eu-mercosur-deal-is-the-agreement-a-threat-to-european-agriculture
4. https://www.independent.ie/business/farming/dairy/milk-production-set-to-increase-by-300m-litres-in-2019-37688456.html
5. https://www.teagasc.ie/media/website/publications/2018/BSAS_Hanrahan_Brexit_Ireland.pdf
6. https://www.agriculture.gov.ie/brexit/tradeandstatistics/
7. https://www.irishtimes.com/news/ireland/irish-news/irish-dairy-industry-moves-out-of-cheddar-over-fears-of-no-deal-brexit-1.3943452
8. http://www.lakeland.ie/news/lakeland-dairies-and-lacpatrick-dairies-merger-creates-co-operative-history
9. https://www.teagasc.ie/media/website/publications/2018/BSAS_Hanrahan_Brexit_Ireland.pdf
10. https://www.irishtimes.com/business/agribusiness-and-food/why-is-the-irish-food-sector-so-exposed-to-a-no-deal-brexit-1.3800197
11. https://www.ifa.ie/brexit/brexit-ireland/
12. https://www.ifac.ie/news/ifac-launch-irish-farm-report-2019/
13. https://www.independent.ie/business/farming/beef/brexit-could-see-beef-farm-incomes-slashed-by-35-forcing-some-to-get-out-of-the-sector-36238943.html
14. https://www.irishtimes.com/business/commercial-property/ireland-has-a-beef-with-eu-mercosur-trade-agreement-1.3371362

About the contributor

Matt O'Keeffe is a long-standing agricultural journalist and farmer from Kilkenny, Ireland. He combines running a 300 cow dairy herd in partnership with his brother, Philip, and nephew, Bill, with editing *Irish Farmers*

Monthly, a magazine aimed at the top dairy, beef, arable and sheep farmers in the country.

He is also an agricultural correspondent, presenter and producer of KCLR's (Kilkenny/Carlow Local Radio) weekly farming programme, *The Farm Show*.

Matt is a former national president of Macra na Feirme, (the Irish Young Farmers' Organisation), former chairman the Irish Farm Apprenticeship Board, and a former vice-chairman of the National Dairy Committee of Irish Farmers' Association.

Chapter 8

Silence of the lambs: How trade deals and tariffs could force Wales' sheep farmers to sell their flocks

Wales' unique landscape is supported by an agricultural sector which is dependent on financial support from — and trade with — the European Union. Huw Thomas, political advisor of NFU Cymru, explains why putting either of those at risk could spell disaster for Wales and its farmers

There's little doubt how critical Wales' farming sector is to the country. It is the cornerstone of a food and drink processing sector worth £7bn to the Welsh economy every year, it supports Wales' unique environment, underpins our rural communities, and provides jobs for five per cent of the country's population.

Almost 90 per cent of Wales' land area is used as agricultural land, with our mild, wet climate and upland landscape the ideal place for growing grass.

It's for this reason that are farming sector is focused on livestock production, with 75 per cent of Wales farmland classified as pastureland — land which is home to a third of the UK's entire sheep population and 11 per cent of the country's cattle[1].

With an economy, landscape and culture so closely tied to agriculture, there's little surprise that farmers are looking towards the outcome of Brexit with some trepidation, as changes to market access and farm support could have major ramifications — the results of which could be felt for generations.

Losing markets but gaining costs

The worst-case scenario for Wales' farmers is that we leave the EU with no deal. Overnight we would immediately lose the favourable access we currently enjoy to the EU 27's markets, and as a third country we could face significant tariffs on our exported produce, with to all intents and purposes could shut us out of European markets.

Wales' farmers are hugely reliant on export markets: about 40 per cent of our lambs are exported, and 95 per cent of them — worth about £300m every year — go to EU customers (*ibid*). As our nearest export market with 500m consumers, it is vital that we don't lose that relationship.

For some sectors like the lamb sector, there will be a degree of protection in that the government has said it will match the EU's tariffs for meat entering the UK from the rest of the world (although we know that New Zealand will continue to enjoy significant tariff-free access to the UK market). But for other sectors, like the beef sector, the tariffs on our exports to the EU will be heftier than the tariffs paid on beef coming in.

With the tariff wall for beef partly dismantled, producers in South America, with their lower costs of production, will be competitive in our marketplace, and will seriously undermine our domestic production base.

The other concern that people often overlook, is there would be non-tariff barriers that would apply to agricultural goods destined for the EU, whether that's more red tape, bureaucracy, border checks that we aren't subject to at the moment. All of those will mean delays and add extra costs to our farmers and food producers.

Dependent on support

Ensuring Wales' farmers are properly supported in a post-Brexit world is also something which is a key focus for us. In Wales, more so than England, direct payments are critical to farm businesses.

Subsidies currently make up more than 80 per cent of farm incomes, with the country's producers receiving over £230m in direct payments through the basic payment scheme.

A further £43m is paid to producers through advanced and entry-level schemes known as Glastir, which pay farmers for managing the land in environmentally-sensitive ways[2].

As so much of Wales' landscape is challenging to manage — some 80 per cent of Wales' grassland pasture is classified as being in Less Favoured Areas[3] — these payments are critical to ensuring farm businesses are able to support the environment and remain profitable.

In July, the Welsh Government announced further details of its plans for a post-Brexit farming policy, which features an integrated programme of support for farmers which will include a sustainable farming payment, alongside business support measures[4].

Working with Welsh Government, we need to ensure a fit-for-purpose future policy which delivers growth for our sector and marks out Wales as a country producing food of the highest quality, underpinned by a strong natural asset base.

Under the CAP our nearest competitors in the EU will continue to receive 70 per cent of their payments as direct support, but without a direct payment in Wales farmers will potentially have to work so much harder to earn that money — something which changes the playing field.

We know that moving from the Common Agricultural Policy to a domestic one will lead to changes, but we have always strenuously made the case for direct payments. We also need to ensure that any changes which are brought in are done so gradually and are properly tested so we know they work before they are rolled out.

More threats than opportunities

If we do crash out of the EU with no-deal or a poor deal, then it could mark the start of some very difficult and uncertain years for many producers, particularly those in the red meat sectors.

Punitive tariffs on exports to the EU could leave priced out of the European market, and we could end up with a massive glut of meat on the domestic market which wouldn't be able to find a home, and that would have an unprecedented impact on farm gate prices.

We saw what happened during the Foot and Mouth crisis in 2001 that cutting markets off can have disastrous consequences. Losing markets in a similar way would cause massive disruption, and we would have to look to government to help mitigate those losses.

First and foremost, we need to secure a favourable trade deal with the EU, our largest and nearest export market. Once that is in place we can start looking at some of the opportunities for Wales' farmers that might lie elsewhere in the world.

We have always articulated concerns about agriculture being used by politicians as a bargaining chip in trade negotiations. As a sector we have to guard against that, and also ensure we have fair and frictionless trade and access to the EU market we so desperately need. The EU is our nearest and most important market, and that won't change.

There has been lots of discussion about opening-up opportunities in other areas of the world, particularly in the Far East. Progress has been slow, and a lot more work is needed to truly secure those markets.

Another area of opportunity could be around public procurement, and if we leave the single market we could look to government to procure more Welsh food into the public sector.

In the past rules in the single market have made this difficult, but similarly the political will to do this has been weak. We always hear of other countries who have found ways to get domestic produce into schools and hospitals, so perhaps it will be an area we can look at again.

Frustration about the future

Ultimately, however, I think the threats outnumber the opportunities, and there is a sense of frustration amongst Welsh farmers about how Brexit is being handled.

Like the general public, Wales' farmers were conflicted, with many wanting to remain and others feeling angry that leaving the EU has been such a drawn-out process.

At the moment there is no clear way forward, and I don't think anyone will look back at this episode and view it as the UK's finest moment.

Ahead of the referendum farmers' biggest concerns were around EU regulation and the way it impinges on farming activity. From sheep tagging to cross compliance and ear tagging cattle, people were frustrated and they wanted to see change.

There were assurances that there would be a bonfire of the regulations and that we would continue to trade with Europe, however it is difficult to see how we can de-regulate and continue to trade with Europe on the same basis: it is one or the other, but not both.

With threats to market access and direct support, it's no exaggeration to say we could see some farmers decide to leave the industry in the coming years.

In the current situation, it's impossible for farmers to prepare themselves for what might lie ahead. Agriculture has long production systems, and if any farmers had been planning for Brexit then they would have been planning for the initial 29 March deadline.

Gestation periods of sheep and cattle aren't things that can be simply moved around, cropping needs to be planned in advance, nature can't be hurried to ripen grain faster, and investments require business plans which are based on long-term finances. The scope for farmers to make no-deal plans really is very limited.

For a lot of farmers, it's a case of waiting and hoping for the best, because they are beholden to so many things that are outside of their control now.

Wales' farmers are passionate about what they do, and they are determined to continue to produce excellent food and protect the environment. But without guarantees for the markets for their produce, there will undoubtedly be some who are thinking long and hard about their future.

Notes
1. https://gov.wales/sites/default/files/statistics-and-research/2018-12/180620-farming-facts-figures-2018-en.pdf
2. http://www.assembly.wales/research per cent20documents/16-053-farming-sector-in-wales/16-053-web-english2.pdf
3. http://www.assembly.wales/research per cent20documents/16-053-farming-sector-in-wales/16-053-web-english2.pdf
4. https://www.fwi.co.uk/news/eu-referendum/new-single-farm-support-scheme-planned-for-wales

About the contributor

Huw Thomas is the political advisor for NFU Cymru, a member organisation which represents farmers and growers in Wales.

Based in Builth Wells, he is responsible for the union's day-to-day contact with members of the Welsh Assembly Government, Welsh MPs and MEPs, with a significant amount of his time now spent working on Brexit issues.

Before joining NFU Cymru is 2004, Huw worked in the civil service for five years. He was born and grew up on a farm in Pembrokeshire.

Chapter 9

A time for environmentally friendly policies?

Leaving the EU offers the chance to create a domestic agricultural policy which not only supports UK farmers, but also the farmed environment. However, with different businesses, ecosystems and political priorities across the UK, can policies which support farming really help the environment? Dr Viviane Gravey examines the challenge

"Enhancing our natural environment is a vital mission for this Government. We are committed to ensuring we leave the environment in a better condition than we found it. And leaving the European Union allows us to deliver the policies required to achieve that – to deliver a Green Brexit. (...).

It means we don't need any longer to follow the path dictated by the Common Agricultural Policy. We can have our own – national – food policy, our own agriculture policy, our own environment policies, our own economic policies, shaped by our own collective interests."

Michael Gove, Oxford Farming Conference, 2018[1]

Among the acrimonious Brexit debates, one issue is proving surprisingly consensual: leaving the Common Agricultural Policy (CAP) and replacing it with a set of policies better suited to UK farmers and to the UK's environment.

From the Green movement, to the Leave campaign and the Government, replacing the CAP is presented as a major Brexit dividend. But how will future UK agriculture policies deliver for the environment?

To understand what is possible to achieve, we need to study how we got there (the CAP and its environmental impacts), to reflect on the various policies already existing (through devolution) and to analyse the environmental credentials of future agriculture policy plans in the UK's four nations.

The past: the EU's Common Agricultural Policy and the environment

The Common Agricultural Policy was set up in the late 1950s with the intent to boost agricultural production in Europe, provide decent incomes for farmers and fair prices for consumers.

In its first three decades, the CAP used a price support system: if agricultural products started trading below a certain politically-agreed price, the European authorities would start to buy up excess production on the European market and subsidise exports on the international market.

This price support system, together with subsidies for access to new technologies, led to a profound intensification of agriculture throughout the continent.

Intensification of agriculture led to a sharp fall in the number of workers in the agricultural sector, and to the number of farms, as smaller ones merged to become larger operations.

According to Eurostat, half a million people worked in farming in the UK in 1973, down to 300, 000 in 2018, while in France over that same period there was a drop from more than two million to 700 000[2].

It saw the rise of monocultures and the creation of larger, more uniform fields with a sharp decline in hedgerows and trees on agricultural land (in France, 75 per cent of hedges were lost over the 20th century [ibid]).

From the late 1970s, environmental impacts of intensification became apparent, with evidence of river and air pollution, soil erosion and a catastrophic drop in the number of farmland birds (-56 per cent between 1970 and 2016 across the UK) and insects, with growing talks of an 'insect armageddon'[3].

In the face of both better understanding of farming impacts on the environment and a growing backlash against the policy, the CAP was reformed repeatedly in the 1990s and 2000s, aiming — amongst other objectives — to foster environmentally-friendly forms of agriculture.

This took two different forms: first, raising the minimum environmental standards for all farmers; and second, making it easier for farmers to go above and beyond and deliver for the environment.

Under the latest 2014-2020 CAP, cross-compliance and the green payment fall under this the first type of environmental support, aiming at raising the baseline, while agri-environment and climate payments fall under this second, more ambitious type.

Critically, despite these policy changes, agriculture in the EU continues to have a negative impact on the environment. Water pollution has, at best, hit a plateau (with growing concerns around pesticides in water supply) and biodiversity loss continues.

This raises key questions for policy-makers in the UK after Brexit: if they are really intent on leaving the environment in a better condition, what do they need to do so they can they succeed where the EU failed?

The present: Before Brexit, how do the four UK nations address environmental challenges?

While the CAP is often criticised as a 'one size fits all' policy, it has become increasingly diverse over the last 20 years, offering member states a menu of options to choose from.

In the UK, this greater flexibility has been seized upon by the four nations. Since devolution in the late 1990s, there are four interpretations of the CAP in the UK. Scotland, Wales, England and Northern Ireland have each made different choices when it comes to supporting environmentally-friendly farming, and so did their closest neighbour, Ireland. This reflects the huge variation in terms of farming conditions and practices across the UK.

For example, Ireland chose to have no minimum claim size, meaning very small farms can receive support. Conversely, there are minimum claim sizes in the UK, with five hectares in England and Wales, and three hectares in Northern Ireland and Scotland.

Ireland and Scotland both re-introduced coupled support, i.e. subsidies directly-linked to production types and levels (in Scotland, this coupled support is for beef calves and hill sheep) but Wales, England and Northern Ireland did not.

Finally, agri-environment-climate payments represent close to 70 per cent of English expenditures on rural development plans, but a much lower proportion in the rest of the UK (21 per cent in Northern Ireland, 25 per cent in Wales, 19 per cent in Scotland) and in Ireland (38 per cent)[4].

These figures on their own are not sufficient to claim that England is the most supportive part of the UK for environmentally friendly agriculture;

this is because different parts of the UK favour different ways of supporting agriculture.

Scotland, for example, offers extensive support to farms in areas facing natural constraints (such as upland areas). Nevertheless, when it comes to the CAP's flagship environment scheme, higher level agri-environment-climate schemes, a stark picture emerges: their uptake in 2017 was much more important in England (with 1.4m hectares) and Scotland (with one million hectares) than Wales (400 000 hectares) and Northern Ireland (100,000 hectares) [5].

The future beyond the CAP – four policies for a green agriculture?

The first Defra secretary after the referendum, Andrea Leadsom, put the emphasis on getting rid of CAP 'red tape', singling out the two policy instruments which define the environmental baseline for farming in the UK: cross-compliance and greening payments[6].

Her successor since June 2017, Michael Gove, adopted a much more environmentally-friendly discourse, putting the idea of 'public money for public goods' at the heart of future policy[7]. This divergence is a stark reminder that once out of the EU, the direction of agricultural policy is likely to change much more frequently and more radically too.

What are the plans for the UK? On funding, we know that farming will continue to be funded at the same level until the end of this Parliament (2022 or before). Between now and then starts a period of 'agricultural transition' in which funds are gradually redirected to new objectives – this transition would end in the late 2020s.

Concerning the environment, we can note some key similarities and divergences between the four nations. First, all four nations favour the use of pilots and trials to test new policy instruments.

Second, all favour a shift towards paying for environmentally-friendly outcomes – for example, increased biodiversity on the farm – more than for specific farming processes. Third, all note the importance of training, advice and peer-to-peer support to help deliver new forms of farming.

But the environment plays different part in the policy proposals. Under Gove, Defra has devised a policy which would gradually reduce direct payments to free 'up £150m for the environment and other public goods' (ibid). These environmental public goods include improving public access, climate change mitigation, improving air, soil and water quality and increasing biodiversity.

The other proposals do not put such emphasis on public goods – conversely, the Welsh, Scottish and Northern Irish proposals are keener on 'keeping farmers on the land and minimising any structural change'[8].

Finally, the proposals vary when it comes to the level of funding for environmental delivery. Currently, EU agri-environment-climate payments are only funded on the basis of reimbursing the extra cost of environmental action (income foregone and additional costs). Both Wales and Northern Ireland argue environmental effort should be more generously supported while these debates are still ongoing in England and Scotland.

The green Brexit crossroads

Agricultural policy in the UK is at a crossroads – while the UK Government is intent on delivering a green Brexit, agricultural policy is a devolved matter. Reviewing existing policies and proposed plans in all four nations reveals different practices and ways of making farming more sustainable – and arguably different levels of ambition for the environment.

Designing future policy in the UK requires a fine balancing act between recognising the incredible variety of the farming sectors, farmland ecosystems and political priorities across the four nations, and making sure there is a level playing field for farmers and no race to the bottom for environmental protection.

Notes

1. https://www.ofc.org.uk/video/rt-hon-michael-gove
2. http://appsso.eurostat.ec.europa.eu/nui/submitViewTableAction.do
3. https://www.theguardian.com/environment/2018/jun/17/where-have-insects-gone-climate-change-population-decline
4. Allen et. al (2014)
   www.niassembly.gov.uk/globalassets/Documents/RaISe/Publications/2014/dard/allen10314.pdf
5. http://jncc.defra.gov.uk/page-4242
6. https://www.gov.uk/government/speeches/environment-secretary-sets-out-ambition-for-food-and-farming-industry
7. https://www.gov.uk/government/news/once-in-a-generation-opportunity-to-shape-future-farming-policy

8. https://ieep.eu/publications/emerging-agricultural-policy-frameworks-in-the-uk

About the contributor

Viviane Gravey is a lecturer in European Politics at Queen's University Belfast.

She holds a PhD in environmental politics from the University of East Anglia, an MSc in Politics and Government of the EU from the London School of Economics, and a Masters in European Affairs from Sciences Po Paris. Her current research focuses on EU environmental policy dismantling, European (dis)integration and the impact of Brexit on the UK environment and agriculture sectors.

As co-chair of the Brexit and Environment network, Viviane offers impartial advice and information on how Brexit is affecting environmental policies and government. She was a lead author of the expert review on the EU referendum and the UK environment1, and has given evidence to the House of Commons, the Welsh Assembly and the Scottish Parliament on what Brexit will mean for the environment and agriculture.

John Mair, Neil Fowler (Editors)

Do They Mean Us?

The Foreign Correspondents' View of Brexit

Written by a range of distinguished foreign journalists, the book explores the spectrum of foreign responses to Brexit, the negotiations, and the outcomes for the UK and its partners.

David Bailey, Alex De Ruyter, John Mair, Neil Fowler (Editors)

Keeping the Wheels on the Road

UK Auto Post Brexit

With just-in-time and huge logistics issues, this book, written by world automotive experts, delves into the outcomes that can be expected post-Brexit and explores the responses that are required.

John Mair, Paul Davies (Editors)

Will the Tory Party Ever Be the Same?

With the Tory Party in turmoil, is this an historic moment for the Tory Party? Leading Tories, with contributions promised from Michael Heseltine, distinguished historians, including Richard Gaunt of Nottingham University, and renowned commentators will provide insights into the likely outcomes.

John Mair, Neil Fowler(Editors)

The Case for Brexit

The Brexiteers, including Patrick Minford and John Redwood, get their voices

Bite-Sized Public Affairs Books are designed to provide insights and stimulating ideas that affect us all in, for example, journalism, social policy, education, government and politics.

They are deliberately short, easy to read, and authoritative books written by people who are either on the front line or who are informed observers. They are designed to stimulate discussion, thought and innovation in all areas of public affairs. They are all firmly based on personal experience and direct involvement and engagement.

The most successful people all share an ability to focus on what really matters, keeping things simple and understandable. When we are faced with a new challenge most of us need quick guidance on what matters most, from people who have been there before and who can show us where to start. As Stephen Covey famously said, "The main thing is to keep the main thing, the main thing."

But what exactly is the main thing?

Bite-Sized books were conceived to help answer precisely that question crisply and quickly and, of course, be engaging to read, written by people who are experienced and successful in their field.

The brief? Distil the 'main things' into a book that can be read by an intelligent non-expert comfortably in around 60 minutes. Make sure the book enables the reader with specific tools, ideas and plenty of examples drawn from real life. Be a virtual mentor.

We have avoided jargon – or explained it where we have used it as a shorthand – and made few assumptions about the reader, except that they are literate and numerate, involved in understanding social policy, and that they can adapt and use what we suggest to suit their own, individual purposes. Most of all the books are focused on understanding and exploiting the changes that we witness every day but which come at us in what seems an incoherent stream.

They can be read straight through at one easy sitting and then referred to as necessary – a trusted repository of hard-won experience.

Bite-Sized Books Catalogue

Business Books

Ian Benn
> Write to Win
>> How to Produce Winning Proposals and RFP Responses

Matthew T Brown
> Understand Your Organisation
>> An Introduction to Enterprise Architecture Modelling

David Cotton
> Rethinking Leadership
>> Collaborative Leadership for Millennials and Beyond

Richard Cribb
> IT Outsourcing: 11 Short Steps to Success
>> An Insider's View

Phil Davies
> How to Survive and Thrive as a Project Manager
>> The Guide for Successful Project Managers

Paul Davies
> Developing a Business Case
>> Making a Persuasive Argument out of Your Numbers

Paul Davies
> Developing a Business Plan
>> Making a Persuasive Plan for Your Business

Paul Davies
> Contract Management for Non-Specialists

Paul Davies
> Developing Personal Effectiveness in Business

Paul Davies
> A More Effective Sales Team
>> Sales Management Focused on Sales People

Lifestyle Books

Anna Corthout
> Alive Again
>> My Journey to Recovery

Anna Corthout
> Mijn Tweede Leven
>> Kruistocht naar herstel

Phil Davies
> Don't Worry Be Happy
>> A Personal Journey

Phil Davies
> Feel the Fear and Pack Anyway
>> Around the World in 284 Days

Stuart Haining
> My Other Car is an Aston
>> A Practical Guide to Ownership and Other Excuses to Quit Work and Start a Business

Stuart Haining
> After the Supercar
>> You've Got the Dream Car – But Is It Easy to Part With?

Bill Heine
> Cancer
>> Living Behind Enemy Lines Without a Map

Regina Kerschbaumer
> Yoga Coffee and a Glass of Wine
>> A Yoga Journey

Gillian Perry
> Capturing the Celestial Lights
>> A Practical Guide to Imagining the Northern Lights

Arthur Worrell
> A Grandfather's Story
>> Arthur Worrell's War

Public Affairs Books

David Bailey, John Mair and Neil Fowler (Editors)
> Keeping the Wheels on the Road – Brexit Book 3
>> UK Auto Post Brexit

Eben Black
    Lies Lobbying and Lunch
        PR, Public Affairs and Political Engagement – A Guide
Paul Davies, John Mair and Neil Fowler
    Will the Tory Party Ever Be the Same? – Brexit Book 4
        The Effect of Brexit
John Mair and Neil Fowler (Editors)
    Oil Dorado
        Guyana's Black Gold
John Mair and Richard Keeble (Editors)
    Investigative Journalism Today:
        Speaking Truth to Power
John Mair and Neil Fowler (Editors)
    Do They Mean Us – Brexit Book 1
        The Foreign Correspondents' View of the British Brexit
John Mair, Alex De Ruyter and Neil Fowler (Editors)
    The Case for Brexit – Brexit Book 2
John Mair, Richard Keeble and Farrukh Dhondy (Editors)
    V.S Naipaul:
        The legacy
John Mills
    Economic Growth Post Brexit
        How the UK Should Take on the World
Christian Wolmar
    Wolmar for London
        Creating a Grassroots Campaign in a Digital Age

Fiction

Paul Davies
    The Ways We Live Now
        Civil Service Corruption, Wilful Blindness, Commercial Fraud, and Personal Greed – a Novel of Our Times
Paul Davies
    Coming To
        A Novel of Self-Realisation
Victor Hill
    Three Short Stories
        Messages, The Gospel of Vic the Fish, The Theatre of Ghosts

Children's Books

Chris Reeve – illustrations by Mike Tingle
        The Dictionary Boy
                A Salutary Tale
Fredrik Payedar
        The Spirit of Chaos
                It Begins

www.ingramcontent.com/pod-product-compliance
Lightning Source LLC
Chambersburg PA
CBHW070429180526
45158CB00017B/942